FAILING TO SUCCESS

"The Definitive Guide to Failing Forward and Learning How to Extract The Greatness Within To Achieve Success. "

By

Christopher Jon Barnett

TABLE OF CONTENTS

INTRODUCTION

Most of us tend to avoid failure. We'd rather see ourselves victorious at the finish line then tending to a damaged ego and attempting to determine where things went wrong. Clear-cut success and triumph offer a cleaner path, while failure is simply a breeding ground for lessons, lessons that can sometimes be tough or even painful to learn. The sweetest victory is the one that's most difficult. The one that requires you to reach down deep inside, to fight with everything you've got, to be willing to leave everything out there on the battlefield—without knowing, until that do-or-die moment, if your heroic effort will be enough. Society doesn't reward defeat, and you won't find many failures documented in history books.The exceptions are those failures that become stepping stones to later success. Such is the case with Thomas Edison, whose most memorable invention was the light bulb, which purportedly took him 1,000 tries before he developed a successful prototype. "How did it feel to fail 1,000 times?" a reporter asked. "I didn't fail 1,000 times," Edison responded. "The light bulb was an invention with 1,000 steps." But the truth is that the most successful people in the world suffered mountains of failure before reaching the pinnacle of success; and it was precisely those failures that prepared them for what would come next.

CHAPTER ONE

WHAT IS FAILURE?

What is failure, really? Why is it so important to fail at something before we can succeed?

It's a word that has a negative connotation affixed to it, but the more that it's understood, the more it can be regarded as something positive. As much talk as there is about failure—fail often, fail forward, etc— there's not nearly as much conversation about what failure actually means. If we say "he failed," all we're really saying is "he didn't succeed." There's no information conveyed other than the fact that something did not happen, that some standards or expectations for success were not met, that something or someone came up short. But the fact that something didn't happen still doesn't explain what did. Failure, therefore, is an incomplete and subjective term. To define failure in any context, you must first ask: what are you falling short of? What standards aren't you reaching? By which metrics are you failing?

You can't truly know what it means to fail if you don't know what it means to succeed. When we think about failure, we think of things in a negative light. We say that failure is painful and that it causes emotional turmoil and upset, and inflicts agonizing pangs of guilt, regret, and remorse. But, for those that have known true failure, and have bounced back from it, understand that failure in life is necessary for success. Sure, failing hurts. In fact, it cuts deep like a razor, slicing its way to our inner core. Yet, it's necessary. And the most successful people in life have failed the most times. If you try to go through life without failing at anything, then you're not really living a life at all. Taking risks and falling down flat on our faces is part of life; it makes us into who we are.

WHY IS FAILURE NECESSARY?

Falling on your face, screwing up or otherwise not handling something well is hard on the ego. It feels terrible when things don't go the way you want, or when a relationship or situation fails because of your own missteps. Even so, the most successful people have a long list of failures. For most of us, failure is a subject we don't find easy to discuss. It's painful, it's disgusting, it's depressing, and in some cases, it's life-threatening even. The bad news is that failure will always be part of life. It's bound to happen and as careful as we would like to be, it is unavoidable.

We've all tasted defeat and we probably will fail more in the coming days and as bad as that may seem, we can't deny the fact that failure has its benefits so instead of seeing failure in a bad light, let's all consider failure as a necessity.

1) **Failure gives meaning to success:**

Do you know why a new personal best time feels so good? It has nothing to do with the numbers themselves. They're just digital lights that pop up on a screen. Objectively, they have no meaning. A personal best time feels so good and those numbers on the board mean something to you because they serve as a representation of the hard work, dedication, sacrifice, and most importantly, persistence through failure that you've gone through to get to that point. In the immediate moment you see that new best time, you feel that rush of euphoria and overwhelming joy because, on a sub-conscious level, you recognize what it took to get that time and the moments of mental and physical pain it took to achieve it. That's why it feels so good. The same is true when you win a medal. It's not the medal itself that brings you happiness. It's just a hunk of metal fastened to a ribbon. The medal represents all of the resilience you showed in fighting through the bad practices, poor meets, and difficult days where you felt like quitting. That's what gives that medal meaning. Without failure, success wouldn't mean anything. It would just be hollow. A time on a board wouldn't hold any significance and a medal around your neck wouldn't make you feel anything. Those things only make you feel something of significance because they serve as a representation of the mental fortitude you showed through the hard times, the difficult moments, the practices where you fell short, and the meets where you weren't your best. Failure is what makes success worth fighting for and achieving.

2) **It helps to deliver some necessary perspective:**

How can you enjoy the view from the top without having crawled your way up from the bottom? Perspective is everything. It allows you to connect with those who are travelling down (or up) the same path that you've traveled and warrants your efforts at guidance—it illustrates your wisdom. More so, perspective from both ends will help you avoid taking future success for granted. If you've succeeded in everything that you've tried on your first attempt, would you fully appreciate your achievements? They would have no meaning and no substance.

3) **Failure is an opportunity to learn:**

When you fail at something, you're ultimately left with two choices: You can succumb to your doubts and fears or you can choose to learn from the experience. By choosing to learn, you can transform your failure into an opportunity to reflect and grow at the very least. You'll always seek to find the positives in a negative situation. It enables you to come out wiser and more adept at overcoming future challenges.

4) **Failure is what keeps you swimming:**

If all you ever did was succeed in swimming, what do you think would eventually happen? If you won every single race you swam in, swam a personal best time in every event, and constantly blew away the competition without ever experiencing any kind of loss or failure, do you know how you'd start to feel? I can tell you – you'd get bored out of your mind. You'd start losing interest in the sport. Why? Because that's how we human beings are designed. We're constantly looking for new challenges, new milestones, and new frontiers. For example, if you were to win a race, how would you prefer to win? Would you prefer it to be a completely boring race with zero challenge where you just blew away the competition without having to put in any real effort? That wouldn't feel any good. It wouldn't mean anything because you didn't even have to test yourself and your abilities. Or, would you prefer to win by being forced to swim to your absolute maximum and barely out-touch the competition to the wall by hundredths of a second? That kind of win always feels so much better. That's because it means something. You had to fight for it. You had to earn it.

5) **The struggle justifies the victory:**

The feeling you get when you achieve something that you've worked so hard to attain—this is what builds a full appreciation for it and what makes your success feel like an actual success. If you've never really failed, you've never really tried. Making that crucial effort allows everything to feel worthwhile at the end, and it lets you know that you've really earned the success that you've worked so hard to achieve. Sometimes it may be more about the journey than the destination, the journey is what may be more influential on our lives and more memorable at the end of the day.

6) Failure is the universe daring you to evolve:

It's a challenge that can crush you or become your greatest opportunity to grow. Nearly all of my personal growth has taken place outside of my comfort zone. Failure provides the ultimate setting for this and has helped many people to decide what they do not want to do.

7) Knowledge:

Failure brings with it important firsthand knowledge. That knowledge can be harnessed in the future to overcome that very failure that inflicted so much pain in the first place. Nothing can replace the knowledge gained from failure. When Thomas Edison famously failed nearly 1,000 times to create a commercially viable electric lightbulb, with each failure, he gained the knowledge of just one more avenue that didn't work. It was the accumulated knowledge developed from nearly 1,000 failed attempts that ultimately led to his success.

8) It helps to redefine your priorities in life:

Failure will either make you or it will break you. But it can't make you until it breaks you. That's the tricky part. No one has experienced a wild sense of success without first failing in a major way. While some have had to endure only a few failures before success, others have endured thousands. But when you fail, something strange happens. You begin to redefine your priorities in life. You reorder the things that matter to you. You look inwards, forcing an inventory of your hopes and your dreams. And you come to realize the things that matter the most to you. For most, this redefinition of priorities is a crucial step for overcoming failure. You shuffle things around to make room for what's important. If success is as important to you as you think, then you begin to make the necessary adjustments.

9) **Failure exposes your weaknesses:**

Everyone has weaknesses, but with self reflection they can be turned into strengths. Being honest with yourself is the first major step that you can take towards personal evolution.

10) **Resilience:**

Failing in life helps to build resilience. The more we fail, the more resilient we become. In order to achieve great success, we must know resilience. Because, if we think that we're going to succeed on the first try, or even the first few tries, then we're sure to set ourselves up for a far more painful failure. The characteristic of resilience can help us in so many ways in life. Resilience helps to breed success by setting the game up to win. Gone are the lofty expectations that thing will happen overnight, and in comes the expectations that true success will take an enormous amount of work and effort.

11) **It makes you more compassionate:**

We all know the power of the mighty ego. Before we fail in a major way, the ego runs your life. You're more concerned with what people think of you or how much money you spend in the face of others. But when you fail, things change. Major failure causes the ego to shatter. As a result, you become more compassionate. You become more in touch with your fellow human beings. It forces you to look deeper at things, understanding and caring more about others rather than solely focusing on your self. The failures in your life can serve you far more than you can ever imagine. They will make you kinder, gentler, and more caring and giving than you can ever be.

12) **Failure makes you want it that much more:**

First off, it'll validate your endeavors. For instance, if you want to become a doctor, fail along the way and still work towards becoming a doctor, then you know for a fact that becoming a doctor is exactly what you're meant to do—that it is your purpose. Secondly, if you fail along the way towards getting what you want, and still want it, your desire for that ambition will grow beyond measure. Failing to do something will re-animate and possibly reinvigorate your ambitions. In other words, if it's something you really want, your thirst for it will grow.

HOW CAN YOU GAIN FROM YOUR FAILURES?

Take a close enough look at any life of note, and you'll quickly discover a legacy of failure. However, it's important to distinguish between failed experiments and failure in the Platonic ideal sense of the word.

Experimental failure happens when you try something, and it doesn't work the way you intended. We've all experienced this brand of failure before. Perhaps you once worked up the courage to ask someone out, and you were turned down. Or, maybe you launched a new product on the market only to be met with utter silence. Regardless of the form it takes, this kind of experimental failure hurts, but it still has a silver lining. These experiences enable us to learn from our mistakes, find new solutions, and grow as individuals.

True failure, in the Platonic sense of the word, isn't something that happens to us. Instead, it's something we choose for ourselves, occurring when we allow the pain of our experimental failures to change our hearts and our minds for the worse. Abraham Lincoln, Thomas Edison, Winston Churchill, Steven

Spielberg, and Albert Einstein; how about Henry Ford? Nobody would argue that these are some of the best, brightest minds to have ever existed and that they've all made tremendous contributions to society. Nobody would ever attach the word failure to any one of them. But that's exactly what they were at one time. Failure is a matter of perspective, plain and simple.

1) **Take the Risk And Pay the Price:**

Nothing ventured, nothing gain. You have to be willing to take the risk venture beyond the comfort zone regardless of what area you are in to gain some form of success. Think about the entrepreneurs, scientists, leaders, and businesses that took the path less trodden and how they were rewarded handsomely. If you are willing to pay the price with the risk you take, then the returns may just surprise you.

2) **Accept failure, but keep trying:**

Michael Jordan once said that, "I can accept failure, everyone fails at something. But I can't accept not trying." Failure then becomes a means to an end, rather than an end in and of itself. In other words, failure is a part of the journey toward success.

Everyone fails at one time or another, the courage part comes in continuing to try.

3) Failing Builds Character:

There is a lesson to be learned from everything, including failing. Perhaps the greatest benefit earned from failure is strength. Think about it: if life were perfect and every endeavor ended in seamless success, what sort of person would you be? The truth is this – failure teaches us more about ourselves and builds character better than success ever could.

4) Remind yourself failure isn't about you as a person:

Failure is about a skill or capability you can build. Take a growth mindset where you don't look at your talent as a stagnant set but as something you can develop, nurture, and strengthen. Changing course is a typical response to failure (after all, some of the subjects did), but if you stick with something and continue trying, it can pay big dividends down the line.

5) Realize Experience Is The Best Teacher:

Think about this, if you do not fail in any of your endeavor, how do you learn to be better? How do you become wiser? People say experience is the best teacher. If you accept that to be true then you need to accept failure as one of the many lessons you gain from experience. So, you get to learn from failure. It's that simple. Think about failure as lessons paid in the journey of life.

6) Continue forward in spite of failure:

Walt Disney was fired because he "lacked imagination and had no good ideas." Here is the man responsible for an empire of imaginative movies and play for children the world over, and yet, he lost his job due to a lack of imagination. The lesson here is to keep moving toward that end goal, even when other people fail to see the same vision.

7) Failure instills courage:

As should be clear by now, most people are scared of failure. Many of us are unwilling to take the uncertain path; we would just prefer to stay in the same boat and not rock it too much. After all, we have responsibilities and people that depend on us. In short, failure requires courage. "If you have made mistakes, even serious ones, there is always another chance for you. What we call failure is not the falling down but the staying down," a quote from Mary Pickford. We are all quite capable of spectacular mistakes and some of us, myself included, have made them. The key is to not allow defeat and failure to be the end-all. You must continue forward. Whether the failure experienced was anticipated or not, you'll need to toughen up a bit to get through it.

8) **Accept it:**

Your failure might have been due to things outside of your control. The system might have also worked against you. But rather than dwelling on those things, you need to focus on how you had a role to play in your failure. The idea that you learn lessons by failing might seem like a cliché to you, but it's familiar because it's right. Learning from success is less automatic—you may be so busy celebrating and taking steps forward, you forget to reflect. Failure provides you with the opportunity to learn and consider how you can strengthen your game for the next go, even if it's under unfavorable conditions.

9) **Success can only grow from failure:**

Benjamin Disraeli, a former British Prime Minister said, "All my successes have been built on my failures." Indeed, failure is only a tipping point when one is on the road to success. Without failure, we as humans don't learn and our movement toward success is stagnated. Let failure guide you toward success instead of becoming the stopping point.

10) **Share your pain:**

Sometimes, sharing your challenges can be a helpful way to build connections. Rather than always putting on a happy face and serving up platitudes, open up to trusted colleagues. They may have advice. What's more, demonstrating vulnerability enables you to build relationships.

CHAPTER TWO

OBSTACLES TO SUCCESS

Everyone wants to succeed in what they do. We all strive for success in our endeavors. And many of us are determined to achieve greatness. As a result, we continuously ask ourselves how we can be more successful. We ponder about the different ways to accomplish success. In our quest for success, we come across many interesting and promising methods. Implementing powerful habits to increase productivity has become second nature to us. However, we tend to ignore one important aspect. It is crucial for success, yet we do not seem to place much emphasis on the question what it is that prevents success. While we are focused on the pursuit of success, we entirely neglect the potential obstacles that stand in between us and our goals. It's ironic. On one hand, we spend a great deal of our time to chase success. On the other hand, we do not always ask ourselves what it is that keeps us from ever accomplishing it. As a result, we are confronted with the same issues over and over again. It's time to bring this to an end. Our life has available and multiples options that ends with best destination. And to reach at we have to know these aforementioned and other sorts of obstacles.

1) **Fear:**

Fear can be both a motivating force, and an obstacle to success. It can keep you from trying and from reaching towards those really big goals. Are you afraid to fail? Analyze the specific situation and force yourself to break the uncomfortable activity into more manageable steps -- or "just deal with it." Identify and utilize every available resource to build upon your strengths and correct your weaknesses. Focus on what could go right and don't obsess about future problems. There's also no reason to unnecessarily call attention to your fears. This will only discourage you, and break down the confidence in others.

Fear can drastically prevent one's growth. It limits us. It makes us accept the ordinary. It stops us from pushing our boundaries. Fear can also hold us back from ever starting to pursue our dreams. If every opportunity and challenge is perceived as too much of a risk, we remain stagnant. We start to pick up bad habits that prevent us from doing what is necessary only because we are too afraid to confront our fears. The fear obstacle comes in many different shapes and forms. In some cases, we are simply afraid of failure. In other cases, we are afraid to be rejected. Yet in other situations we simply do not want to be confronted with the unknown. Whatever it is, it holds us back from being successful. When it comes to the pursuit of your dreams, you have to be willing to take risks. If you always do what you've always done, you will always get what you've always got. Fear can stand right in-between you and success. It can prove to be quite a disadvantage if you haven't learned to face and conquer our fears. Consider failure as an essential learning experience. It's a challenge for you to try even harder to succeed at what you're doing. Understand that failure simply cannot be avoided. So try to make the best out of each and every one of your failures. It might be painful to be knocked down to the ground, but in the long run you will benefit tremendously from it, if you're willing to use your failures as stepping stones to success.

What scares you? Learning how to overcome fears of failure can be challenging for everyone. Fortunately, all fears are learned. No one is born with fears. Fears can therefore, be unlearned by practicing self-discipline repeatedly with regard to fear until it goes away. The most common fears that we experience, which often sabotage all hope for success, are the fear of failure, poverty, and loss of money. These fears cause people to avoid risk of any kind and to reject opportunity when it is presented to them. They are so afraid of failure that they are almost paralyzed when it comes to taking any chances at all. Common ways of facing your fears are explained below:

• **Understand fear and embrace it:**

Fear exists to keep us safe. It is not inherently bad or good but a tool we can use to make better decisions. Fear isn't designed to keep us inactive, but to help us act in ways that generate the results we need and want. Embrace fear as instruction and let it inform your actions, but not control them.

• **Evaluate Risks:**

Sometimes, fear comes from simply not knowing very much about the thing you fear. For example, you might be afraid of airplanes because it seems like you have heard about a lot of in-air incidents that lead to injury or death. However, if you look into the statistics, you might learn that the probability of death on a U.S. commercial jet airline is 1 in 7 million (in comparison to 1 in 600 from smoking). You can also learn more about what causes those bumps and jolts during turbulence on an aircraft—it's simply the movement of air having an effect on the aircraft and, if you're buckled in properly, poses very little threat to you. Of course, less tangible fears, such as being afraid of public speaking, don't necessarily have statistics to help you learn more about the risks you perceive. But you can read about other people's successful public speaking ventures, or learn more about the successful public speaking strategies, to help you feel more confident.

• **Don't just do something, stay there:**

We tend to admire people who are quick to action, but being deliberate, creating a plan, and pacing yourself are also actions. Many a successful undertaking has been threatened or ruined by haste alone. When fear strikes consider whether the correct action might be to analyze the options and make a wise, well thought out choice rather than jumping to what seems right in the heat of the moment.

• **Create an Action Plan:**

The key to facing your fears is to take one small step at a time. Going too fast or doing something too scary before you are ready can backfire. But it's also important to keep moving forward. A moderate amount of anxiety is ok. Don't wait for your anxiety to disappear before taking a step forward, or you may find yourself waiting for a change that isn't going to come on its own. Name the fear. Sometimes merely stating what your fear is gives you the strength to deal with it. Say your fear out loud, write it down, or focus your mind on it. When you try to ignore your fear, it grows. When you face it, it shrinks.

• Try Seeing a Therapist:

If your fears are debilitating, you aren't having much success facing them on your own, or your fear may is related to a specific health condition, like an eating disorder, social anxiety disorder, or PTSD, you can seek the help of a trusted mental health professional. If you have a specific phobia, which is a persistent, diagnosable anxiety disorder, you may not feel prepared to conquer your fears on your own. A cognitive behavioral therapist can help desensitize you to your fears one small step at a time.

• Educate yourself:

We are afraid of nothing so much as the unknown. If your fear is based on a lack of information, then get the information or knowledge you need to examine the situation based on facts rather than speculation.

• **Visualize success:**

Athletes may imagine the successful completion of a physical task thousands of times before achieving it. This mental mapping ensures that when the body moves, it's more likely to follow its pre-ordained path. The same practice will prepare you to succeed at whatever you're trying to achieve.

2) **Uncertainty:**

Experiencing uncertainty is different than taking a risk. Risk involves a known probability that something will or will not happen; uncertainty, however, indicates the probabilities are unknown. Therefore, we cannot predict an outcome. How many of us have missed tremendous opportunities and experiences because we've chosen to walk away when faced with uncertainty? When we avoid challenges because we're scared of failure, it's a form of self-sabotage. We've held on to a self-limiting belief about what we can do in life. Mental toughness is the ability to break unproductive patterns of behavior. It is managing your emotions, thoughts and behavior in ways that will set you up for success. In today's world, the risk of failure is all around us and uncertainty abounds. Even when we have enticing career opportunities, we are often too afraid to take them because we don't want to risk losing a stable income. However, some people refuse to accept this and learn how to deal with uncertainty, and there are many techniques to tackle it. When we master uncertainty, we can expand our mental capabilities and have the energy to fully commit to new ideas and inventions. Shortly,you will learn what uncertainty does to us, why we are so scared of it, and find out about the tools you need to deal with it:

• **Learn how to overcome innate fear of brain uncertainty:**

Our thinking cerebral brain and our emotional limbic brain are hardwired to react with fear when confronted with uncertainty. Neuroeconomics is the study of how our brains shape our economic behavior and it seeks to explain savings trends, stock market fluctuations, consumer confidence, etc. A study by a Caltech neuroeconomist used a brain scan to show which parts of the brain are active when people engage in gambling -- similar to the gambles taken in business on a regular basis. It turns out that the less information the subjects of the study had to go on, the more irrational their decisions. Common sense might nudge you to think that the opposite to be true: The less information we have, the more careful and rational we become in the decisions we make. Not so.

Neuroeconomists explain that as the uncertainty of the scenarios increased, the limbic system took control of the slower thinking cerebral brain. The limbic system engenders emotions such as anxiety and fear. In the caveman days, this response kept us safe from saber-toothed tigers. In modern life, it hinders our ability to overcome uncertainty in both business and life. Since uncertainty makes your thinking brain yield control to your emotional limbic system, you need to engage your rational brain if you plan to overcome the unpredictability of modern life and the anxiety it produces.

• **Stay positive:**

Positive thoughts calm fear and irrational thinking by focusing your brain's attention on something that is completely stress-free. You have to give your wandering brain a little help by consciously selecting something positive to think about. Any positive thought will do to refocus your attention.

When things are going well and your mood is good, this is relatively easy. When you're stressing over a tough decision and your mind is flooded with negative thoughts, this can be a challenge. In these moments, think about your day, and identify one positive thing that happened, no matter how small. If you can't think of anything from the current day, reflect on the previous day or days or even the previous week, or perhaps you're looking forward to an exciting event. The point here is that you must have something positive that you're ready to shift your attention to when your thoughts turn negative due to the stress of uncertainty.

• **Never confuse memories with facts:**

We can overcome uncertainty to become successful if we recognize that our recollection of the past is not always accurate. Our memories are fallible, and yet we often treat them as more reliable than current observation or data. Our memory does not store information exactly as it's presented to us. Instead, we extract the gist of the experience and store it in ways that makes the most sense to us. That's why different people witnessing the same event often have different versions. Psychologists have found that once we've formed a viewpoint, we embrace information that confirms that point of view and ignore, or reject, information that is contrary to it. Confirmation bias suggests that we pick out bits of data that make us feel good because they confirms our own opinions. The same applies to our memories. If we have a self-limiting belief about what we can do, we hold on to memories that confirm our low self-esteem. Our memories are not always fact; instead, they can be forms of self-deception if we're not careful.

• **You know what you know and what you don't:**

When uncertainty makes a decision difficult, it's easy to feel as if everything is uncertain, but that's hardly ever the case. People who excel at managing uncertainty start by taking stock of what they know and what they don't know and assigning a factor of importance to each. They gather all the facts they have, and they take their best shot at compiling a list of things they don't know, for example, what a country's currency is going to do or what strategy a competitor will employ. They actually try to identify as many of these things as possible because this takes away their power.

• **Learn how to become more agile in your thinking:**

Successful people prepare for all possible outcomes. If you are smart, you will always test the ground before taking a step into the unknown. That is not lack of confidence; that is old-fashioned self-preservation. This is not the same as "expect the worst" because it's reminding yourself that you can handle whatever difficulty comes along. Ask yourself, "What is the worst that can happen?" It is a powerful question because it prepares you for the worst so you can plan how you'd handle it. This question challenges us to look at all possibilities. When we do, we expand our ability to cope and adapt to different situations, thereby making uncertainty look more manageable.

• **Focus only on what matters:**

Some decisions can make or break your company. Most just aren't that important. The people who are the best at making decisions in the face of uncertainty don't waste their time getting stuck on decisions where the biggest risk is looking foolish in front of their co-workers. When it comes down to it, almost every decision contains at least a small factor of uncertainty—it's an inevitable part of doing business. Learning to properly balance the many decisions on your plate, however, allows you to focus your energy on the things that matter and to make more informed choices. It also removes the unnecessary pressure and distraction caused by a flurry of small worries.

3) **Self-doubt:**

Many people think the difference between success and failure is a combination of luck, talent and resources. But experts say success depends much more on our complex brain processes and how we harness them. The good news is that success is within our reach. Research in science, psychology and education shows that self-doubt and fear—powerful impediments to progress—can be overcome with focus, careful practice and knowledge of brain chemistry. Our brains can change over time, for the better. Knowing that doubt is one of many normal human emotions running through our brains, learning how to manage and transcend any negative feelings is the key to overcoming self-doubt. Life metaphorically is best described as continuously transitioning through each of the four seasons: winter, spring, summer and fall. Truly successful people are not those who try to avoid certain seasons, but rather are those who choose to embrace, overcome and thrive as they seamlessly flow between seasons, regardless of how long or difficult each one may be. Successful people just don't overcome the difficult season of winter. They thrive during the harsh cold; they blossom throughout the spring, reap a lush harvest during the summer and adequately prepare for the fall and winter that inevitably follow. Such cyclical expectations and preparations are mindsets that are key to sustaining against-the-odds success. You don't have to continue to live like this. You can overcome self-doubt and find the success that you long for. Here's how:

- **Find Someone To Talk To:**

  The first step in overcoming self-doubt if talking to a professional. Many people are leery of taking this step because there is a stigma that surrounds mental health issues. However, self-doubt brings down your quality of life. When you get the help that you need you will be able to take on new experiences and risks in life and start living the life you have dreamed of. A professional can help you walk the path to believing in yourself and trusting yourself again.

- **Know you're not alone:**

First, acknowledge that everyone has doubts. It's isolating to believe that you're the only one suffering from a lack of confidence. You'll sabotage your success if you feel like an outlier.

- **Limit The Amount Of Time You Spend With Negative People:**

Spend time with positive people. The last thing you need when struggling with self-doubt is to be around negative people that are going to pull you down. Reduce the amount of time that you spend with people that always see what's bad in a situation. Seek to spend time with the people that are always optimistic. Their good attitude and hope will begin to rub off on you. Be careful not to share too much information with people that are negative. When you share an idea that you have with people that are overly negative, they are going to point out every single problem that they can think of, even if they don't know what they are talking about. They usually try to tell you that they are "just trying to help," but you feel like they are doing the exact opposite. These people often don't to bring you down, but they are most likely struggling with self-doubt as well that keeps them stuck in the place where they are. If you want to rise above that, you need to spend time with other people that are succeeding and taking chances in life. Keep the people who encourage you close and seek out their feedback on a regular basis. Distance yourself from individuals who are always pessimistic toward you, your business and your future prospects.

- **Get in motion:**

In physics, Newton's First Law of Motion states that an object at rest will stay at rest until some unbalanced force acts upon it. Similarly, an object in motion will remain in motion unless an unbalanced force acts upon it. To overcome paralyzing self-doubt, get in motion. Take one small (even tiny, if necessary) step forward to start building momentum. For example, if you want to write a book, quiet self-doubt by writing just 50 words. It will take you less than two minutes to complete the task. And then once you've written 50 words, you will start to feel your resistance to write die down and you can keep going.

- **Don't Worry About Everyone Else:**

If you struggle with self-doubt you probably also struggle with feeling like other people are judging you. We tend to think that people care about what we are doing far more than they actually do. In reality, most people are so concerned with their own lives that they aren't really paying that close of attention to what you are doing. So, if you spend your time worrying about what others are thinking of you, it's time to stop. You feel your best when you are true to yourself. Stop worrying about what everyone else is thinking or what they will think if you decide to go in a certain direction they don't agree with. You will never please everyone all of the time, but as long as you are trying to the one person, you will not please is yourself. Do not look to others for your confidence, instead work on building true confidence from seeing the success in your life. You do not need others to validate your opinions or ideas.

- **Distract yourself:**

It's all too easy to become overly caught up in negative thoughts, which left unchecked can spread to all aspects of your life. Break the cycle immediately. A few ways to try to exit this self-destructive mental loop include taking a walk, moving on to another project or doing exercise. Experiment and find the technique that works best to quell pessimism before it consumes you.

CHAPTER THREE

ATTITUDE

Life doesn't always go the way you want it to, right? Whether it's a minor inconvenience like unexpected traffic or a major setback in your career, relationships or health, one thing is certain. Much of our success and fulfillment comes down to how we see things. It comes down to the meaning we choose to give the events and circumstances we find ourselves in. It comes down to what we believe this one, precious life is all about. Your energy is contagious. So think about what you want people to catch from you. Your attitude impacts everything. It directs your thoughts, your energy and most of all, the actions you take. use more of your intelligence. To become aware of how much power you have in this area and take responsibility for the impact your attitude has on the quality of your life, and on others. Because the actions you take, the energy you exude and therefore — the results you create are vastly different when you have a positive attitude rather than a negative one. While that might seem obvious, most people just react to the world around them and allow their attitude to be dictated by their ever-changing circumstances. Look. Even if you have good intentions, do the right things, and work really hard, if you don't also have this energetic skill mastered, this ability to maintain and express a genuine positive attitude, you're not going to be as successful or fulfilled as you deserve to be.

WHAT IS ATTITUDE?

In psychology, an attitude refers to a set of emotions, beliefs, and behaviors toward a particular object, person, thing, or event. Psychologists define attitudes as a learned tendency to evaluate things in a certain way. This can include evaluations of people, issues, objects, or events. Such evaluations are often positive or negative, but they can also be uncertain at times. Attitudes are often the result of experience or upbringing, and they can have a powerful influence over behavior. While attitudes are enduring, they can also change. An individual's attitude is his perception of the world around him, a perception that affects the way he thinks, act, and feel. Some people think that their present attitude is influenced by their current situation. If the situation is good, then they are in a positive mood. If not, then that explains their negative attitude. We use our circumstances as an excuse for our behavior. Truth is, attitudes are developed and shaped by our experience, and over time, they turn into habits. But, this can be changed with the right knowledge. Your situation affects your emotions, and you have a choice whether you remain positive or let your negative emotions get the better of you. Everybody goes through difficult times but many people are able to take control of themselves. You can still have a great day even if you are facing challenging times. No matter how bad your situation is, you can still find something to be thankful for. The question is whether you are willing to find ways to still feel good or just let your circumstances affect you and ruin your day.

- **Attitude Formation:**
  There are a number of factors that can influence how and why attitudes form. Here is a closer look at how attitudes form.
- **Experience:**
  Attitudes form directly as a result of experience. They may emerge due to direct personal experience, or they may result from observation.
- **Social Factors:**

Social roles and social norms can have a strong influence on attitudes. Social roles relate to how people are expected to behave in a particular role or context. Social norms involve society's rules for what behaviors are considered appropriate.

- **Learning:**

Attitudes can be learned in a variety of ways. Consider how advertisers use classical conditioning to influence your attitude toward a particular product. In a television commercial, you see young, beautiful people having fun on a tropical beach while enjoying a sports drink. This attractive and appealing imagery causes you to develop a positive association with this particular beverage.

- **Conditioning:**

Operant conditioning can also be used to influence how attitudes develop. Imagine a young man who has just started smoking. Whenever he lights up a cigarette, people complain, chastise him, and ask him to leave their vicinity. This negative feedback from those around him eventually causes him to develop an unfavorable opinion of smoking and he decides to give up the habit.

- **Observation:**

Finally, people also learn attitudes by observing people around them. When someone you admire greatly espouses a particular attitude, you are more likely to develop the same beliefs. For example, children spend a great deal of time observing the attitudes of their parents and usually begin to demonstrate similar outlooks.

HOW CAN YOUR ATTITUDE INFLUENCE YOUR SUCCESS?

Your attitude has a profound impact on the way you lead people. It affects the way you sell and the way you serve customers. Your attitude has a direct impact on how you communicate and collaborate with others, how you contribute to the culture of your work environment, and how you perform your daily tasks and responsibilities. Ultimately, your attitude shapes your success and your happiness. Other things being equal, the person with the best attitude will win. Other things not being equal, the person with the best attitude usually wins. Unfortunately, many people cling to beliefs and attitudes that restrict rather than empower their performance.

1) **Positive Attitude Brings About Positive Health:**

When you're stuck in a rut, often the first thoughts that run through your head are negative, thus your outlook likely becomes pessimistic. But, if you can transform those thoughts into more positive ones, then you're on your way to talking yourself out of that rut, which allows you to move forward. Of course, positive thinking doesn't mean ignoring all the bad or unpleasant feelings altogether. It just means that you approach unpleasantness in a more positive and productive way–instead of taking everything as a victim to negative circumstances, you see it as an opportunity to learn and grow. These automatic thoughts can be positive or negative. Some of your self talk comes from logic and reason, while other self talk may arise from misconceptions that you create. Others could come from external sources such as negative people around you, or messages from the media. The key is to surround yourself with positive influences that can help turn those negative thoughts into positive, more productive actions.You'll not only feel better about the situation, but in the long run, positive thinking can lower your levels of distress and depression and give you better coping skills during hardships.

2) **Effects Toward Your Life:**

Living life requires a predominantly positive attitude due to its nature of high and low cycle. Few people, if any, remain at the top their whole lives. It is unavoidable that one will undergo phase of trials and tribulations. Even before any difficulty happens, a person's mindset must be able to possess a certain level of positivity and realism. Although nobody can ever have absolute control in what occurs throughout their life, the attitude and approach they choose in handling life's obstacles is fully within control.

3) Suffering is Inevitable, So It's Best to Accept It:

Now, one thing that everyone goes through at some point, is suffering. It's a harsh reality, yet you can't actually avoid it. We experience suffering as the result of unhappiness, fear, anger, loss or frustration. In fact, it would be hard to even imagine the feeling of happiness if we never experienced suffering! How would we ever compare it? So instead of wallowing in sorrow about the suffering you have endured, take the suffering as an opportunity for change. Did you get laid off from your job? Perhaps this would be a good time to re-assess your career goals. Rather than feeling negative and stuck, use your time and energy to find opportunities which will put you ahead. With the right attitude, anything can seem possible.

3) **Forming the Right Attitude:**

Our attitude about any state or condition in our life is always within our power to choose. Attitudes are rooted in one's own beliefs and are unique across most individuals. They do not form overnight but rather, throughout the course of one's life. Moreover, certain attitudes create a negative impact to one's life and may even cause it to fall apart. This is why it is an important task for each person to help themselves take on the proper attitude direction. Do remember that a person whose heart is not in what he or she is doing will never be half as productive as someone who has the right attitude. It is simple really, a positive attitude produces much more favorable results while negative attitudes only serve to generate failure. We all have within us the power to respond to any given situation in any way we want regardless of the circumstances and this is why you can either choose to react positively or negatively.

4) **Gratitude Goes a Long Way in Shaping Attitude:**

Now, this may seem difficult to do when you're already feeling down, but having gratitude is a very useful when you're trying to navigate your way out of a setback. Being grateful for existing accomplishments and the supports in your life will help you see them more clearly, build your own confidence, and give you a better overall outlook on what your limitations really are and what you have to do to overcome them. With a grateful attitude, you limit the damage of negative influences, and strengthen the impact of positive ones. Being grateful, even during the toughest of times, steers your attitude towards a more positive one, allowing you to get back on your feet much more quickly. Many studies done on gratitude have shown positive results for people who practice regularly, such as improvement in relationships and in mental health. There's even studies that show higher motivation in work settings due to a simple 'thank you' from managers to their subordinates.

5) Learning and Unlearning Attitudes:

Much like walking, writing, playing sports and acquiring any other skill, attitude can also be learned. Having already mentioned that attitude develops from one's own personal experiences and interactions throughout life, we have already accumulated several different attitudes on different things or instances which can be both negative and positive. It is important to recognize a negative attitude right away as it hinders growth and success. Much like how we can learn them, we are also able to unlearn them and develop new and more positive ones.

6) **Your Attitude Sets the Tone for Success:**

Do you see the importance of having a positive attitude? It is so much more than a mindset or state of mind. Your attitude sets the tone for every action and behavior that follows after, and that will determine how long it takes for you to break free from your current circumstance. So if you're currently in an unhappy situation, why not give it a try and look at things from a more positive outlook? As mentioned, not only does having a positive attitude bring about favorable outcomes, it also brings about positive health in the long run. Embracing hardship as it is, and using it as a learning experience to grow, will also make you stronger. And, whether you're going through good or bad times, practicing gratitude will no doubt help to limit the damage of negative influences and strengthen the impact of positive ones.

CHAPTER FOUR

NO QUICK PATH

Ever wonder why so many smart people get scammed? It's not a lack of intelligence that leads people into scams, it is a desire to get more than they've earned. Many of us have a sense that we were born for greatness. But most of us, by circumstances and the general difficulty of life, are held down all our lives, and never reach our greatness. If we see a few people who don't seem to be held down (usually a public relations scam), we either envy them or seek to emulate them. At some point, we get so frustrated, and want greatness so badly, that we'll take almost any path to it. The quick path to greatness is always a fraud. It doesn't matter whether you are seeking financial greatness, religious greatness, or some other form of greatness; the path that appeals to you when you are frustrated and disappointed with life is not a good one. Success doesn't happen by accident. Success happens when you decide what you want, you make a plan to go after it and; you follow through on the plan until you have created the result you are after. That may sound familiar; there is one key point in that which escapes most people – you decide what you want. You are the one who must determine your path to success because it is you who must decide what constitutes success in your life. There are billions spent around the world each year by people who are desperately trying to become more successful. They focus on strategies but fail to realise that strategies cannot help them if they do not really know what they want. You cannot walk your path to success until you have built that path and; you cannot build your path to success until you know your desired destination.

HOW DO YOU KNOW YOU ARE ON THE RIGHT PATH TO SUCCESS?

The path to success does not look the same for every person. However, there are milestones for success that are common on everyone's paths. These are milestones that let you know that you're on to something amazing. People often tend to make the same mistakes on their paths to success which block the road ahead. There's a certain sense of ease when you're heading in the right direction that doesn't feel like it needs to be questioned. You just go with the flow effortlessly and without hesitation because things just seem to be working out as they should. Some people describe it as having a sense of just knowing that things are the way they are supposed to be. But even if you're on the right track, sometimes you may feel like your life is going nowhere, and end up with very little energy and no real motivation in things that you used to be motivated in. Below are list of signs that you are on the right path to success:

1) **You've learned from your experiences:**

The road of life although well-trodden is no smooth ride, but it's worth it. No matter how bad a situation is, there is always one thing you can take away — a lesson. Reflect on your success and your defeat. Remember those things that when you first attempted or even after trying repeatedly that are now second nature. Everything happens for a reason and they have all contributed to where you are and who you are today. Endeavor to let your successes and defeats, bolster you for those to come. Think about what you've been through and what you've been able to do and pat yourself on the shoulder.

2) **Things start aligning for you:**

When you're on a course that's taking you where you want and need to be, it can be as if the universe starts sending you what you need to accomplish your goals. People or events show up to support and further your cause. Required money comes in from a donation or an unexpected source. Things just seem to fall into place and work out. Oftentimes, it feels like a mere coincidence or even a miracle; and maybe it is, but if you're experiencing this, why question it?

3) **Things are getting tough:**

Is life feeling like a constant uphill battle that seems to bring on challenge after challenge? Do you see roadblock after roadblock with no signs of them stopping anytime soon? When we are on the right path and moving towards our goals and desires. The Universe can begin throwing curve balls and situations that challenge us. This helps us focus on developing the skills we need to succeed. The late nights and tedious jobs are only making you stronger and teaching you more. If everything was easy, you would never want to move anywhere in life and you'd constantly find yourself going nowhere. Remember, sometimes it's the darkest before the dawn. Don't give up.

4) **You have a zest for knowledge:**

With online tools at your fingertips, you can learn about anything you want to. This learning can take place at your own pace wherever it is convenient to you. Make the best use of all the opportunities to learn that come your way. Truly successful people have to be knowledgeable, at least in the area of their expertise. The wider your knowledge base, the better for you. Remember success is first measured in the things money cannot buy and knowledge and the desire for knowledge are two of those

5) You don't allow obstacles to stop you:

Being on the right path doesn't mean everything will automatically and magically fall into place 100 percent of the time. But when obstacles do arise, you'll often find yourself diving right in and coming up with creative solutions on how to overcome or work around them. Consider an opposite situation: have you ever been in a miserable job or a horrible, failing relationship that you absolutely knew you wanted to leave? Think about how thrilled you'd have been if an opportunity had shown up that provided you with a perfect excuse to make an easy escape. If you're on the right path at the right time, obstacles that show up become nothing more than bumps in the road and the idea of giving up won't feel like the right option. You'll be driven from within to find another way to make it work so you can continue on towards your dream.

6) You're forgetting about the past:

The past. While nice to think about from time to time. It can anchor us to our PAST experiences. When you start to find yourself always looking FORWARD. Thinking about the next two, three, and even four steps in your plan you will start to feel freer and closer to your dreams. The Universe is listening to you and your call for help moving forward. It is recognizing that you are moving towards your goals and cutting all ties to the anchors of the past that are holding you back.

7) You have good qualities:

Love, the ability to forgive, kindness, mildness, self-control are all some of the qualities that lead to true success. You may not build that empire by being very kind but you'll feel good about yourself and whatever you are able to achieve especially when you see the smile on other people's faces when you have been able to share with them. Being able to forgive keeps you sane. It is also a sign of great strength. It demonstrates your ability to shed unnecessary weight even if it is only for your sake. If you are able to forgive yourself you won't stay in the haze of thinking you're unsuccessful for very long.

8) Decision-making seems easier when you're on the right path:

Deciding between two options or what your next best steps should be is often easy (or at least easier) when you're on the right track. Even if you're unaware of it, heading in the right direction and feeling good about it usually means that you've tapped into, and are able to access, your intuition. This allows you to clearly see and feel what will work best for you without an excessive amount of struggle or effort.

9) You feel at peace:

When we're moving along a path that isn't really right for us or is moving us further away from our dreams, we can often feel agitated and stuck. We can't sleep. We find ourselves playing the victim. And we constantly want to be somewhere else. But. When you notice that this sinking feeling has been swapped with a feeling of peace, recognize that it is the Universe telling you that you're on the RIGHT path. Use this new-found sense of peace and security to fuel your work and BECOME the successful person you know you can be. Don't let anything take it away from you.

10) There's no need to compromise your morals or beliefs:

When you're choosing the right path in life for you and your soul, you won't feel like you're selling out, or doing things that you'll later have to apologize for or regret. When you can stand in confidence about your decisions and actions, without having to make excuses, you know you're heading in the right direction.

CHAPTER FIVE

WHAT ARE YOU PASSIONATE ABOUT?

If you ask any successful person to describe their journey, they will be able to pinpoint failures that were, in most cases, the launching pad to what they consider their successes. Success, as I've mentioned before, is not just monetary. Success is so much more than that. It's the feeling of fulfillment that you get when you achieve what you set out to do. It's important to recognize this because it's easy to set financial goals and focus on the wrong target. Ask any millionaire - money is great...absolutely. But it doesn't provide the inner feeling of fulfillment that keeps you moving. Successful people, ie: fulfilled and happy people, do two things right that we can all learn a lot from.

- They approach passion in the right way

- They except and even embrace failures

The most important ingredient in achieving your goals is passion. "Signing on" to something that you are passionate about can take you just about anywhere. Intelligence, connections and courage may all help, but nothing can trump passion. The truly successful person is almost always one who is extremely passionate about his or her endeavor. There are many standards used to define "success." Some people measure success by the size of a person's bank account. Others measure it based upon a person's power or influence. And still others measure success by one's level of happiness or joy in life. The important thing is not money, but rather doing something that you really love to do. With this in mind, it is best to set goals around something you like. By identifying your interests and hopefully your passions, you can set goals that are important to you and then have fun in the process of actually achieving them.

HOW TO KNOW YOUR PASSION?

If you want to be fulfilled, happy, content, and experience inner peace and ultimate fulfillment, it's critical that you learn how to find your passion and life purpose. Without a life purpose as the compass to guide you, your goals and action plans may not ultimately fulfill you.

1) **Clear out the distractions:**

One reason you may not know your passion: you haven't given yourself the time and space to pursue it. Now, many of the distractions in our lives — picking up kids from daycare, writing a proposal for work, dealing with a burst pipe in the basement — are non-negotiable; they come with being a human in the world. But what about the negotiable distractions? One major source is right there in your pocket: your phone. "Whether it's watching frivolous videos or scrolling through social media, there's enough that you could do those things forever.

2) **Never Quit Trying:**

Can't find your passion at first? Give up after a few days and you're sure to fail. Keep trying, for months on end if necessary, and you'll find it eventually. Thought you found your passion but you got tired of it? No problem! Start over again and find a new passion. There may be more than one passion in your lifetime, so explore all the possibilities. Found your passion but haven't been successful making a living at it? Don't give up. Keep trying, and try again, until you succeed. Success doesn't come easy, so giving up early is a sure way to fail. Keep trying, and you'll get there.

3)Think of what you loved to do as a child:

This is probably the simplest way to unearth what pursuits hold the potential to light up your days. Before the grown-ups get to us with their ideas, most of us know exactly who we are and what would make us happiest. Were you obsessed with horses? Maybe you should head to a dude ranch for your next vacation. Loved finger painting or drawing? Sign up for an art class. Sang at the top of your lungs until people begged you to stop? Think about joining a local choir (or starting your own garage band!)

4) Brainstorm:

Nothing comes to mind right away? Well, get out a sheet of paper, and start writing down ideas. Anything that comes to mind, write it down. Look around your house, on your computer, on your bookshelf, for inspirations, and just write them down. There are no bad ideas at this stage. Write everything down and evaluate them later.

5) Ask Yourself: Is There Something You Already Love Doing?

Do you have a hobby, or something you loved doing as a child, but never considered it as a possibility? Whether it's reading comic books, collecting something, making something, creating or building, there is probably a way you could do it for a living. Open a comic book shop, or create a comic book site online. If there's already something you love doing, you're ahead of the game. Now you just need to research the possibilities of making money from it.

6) Question your answer:

We often declare something we want but can't figure out how to get it or why we're having trouble getting it. What we think is the answer may in fact only be the starting point, a question that needs to be peeled back to discover another layer of the onion. We want a new job. We want to be promoted. We declare these statements as our goals but get stuck in achieving them. Instead, consider the why. Why a new job? Why a promotion? What is the root issue behind the declaration? Perhaps we don't really want a new job, but we're seeking growth and meaning in our work that we're not currently finding. Is a new job the only solution or are there other things we can try without leaving our current job? Reframing the issue can help unpack the real question and help us move forward.

7) **Stop trying:**

Even though it seems everyone gets a prize for effort and participation these days, trying and trying and trying sometimes seem like Sisyphus rolling the stone up the hill, only to have it roll back down. We may be expending too much energy on "trying" but not actually doing. Imagine you want to go skydiving. Standing on the airplane doorway with your parachute ready to go is evidence of really trying. But if you never jump, you're never actually skydiving. You're just trying. You could spend days and months and years, and a lot of money making the attempt. But no matter how many times you go up on that airplane, no matter how many different packs you put on, and no matter how many instructors you have, you will never sky dive until you jump. Jump.

CHAPTER SIX

YOUR WHY

Never go into business for yourself without having a 'why.' If your sole purpose for wanting to become an entrepreneur is to make millions of dollars, your chances of success will be slim to none. It would be recommend going into finance, instead. As an entrepreneur, when the journey gets difficult (and it definitely will), when you're making painful sacrifices, and damaging personal relationships in the pursuit of making your dreams come true, the one thing you will always need to fall back upon is your 'why'. What's your greater purpose for wanting to start a business? Do you want to become successful, so that you can in turn lift others out of poverty? Are you working on a solution that'll serve to make the lives of others genuinely better? Be super honest with yourself when you're trying to find your purpose in business. The opportunities you'll be most likely to stick with, are the ones which you're personally invested in. The problems you're passionate about solving.

WHY FOLLOWING YOUR PASSION LEADS TO YOUR PURPOSE?

Your purpose is the reason you explore through life and your passion is the fire that lights the way. If you can't work out your purpose right now, it's okay; follow your heart – your passion. Your passion will lead you right into your purpose.Why Pursue your Passion? People speak about pursuing passion all the time, but what does it really mean? Does it mean quitting your day job and turning what you love to do into a career? The response would be: maybe! It's important for you to love what you do and feel inspired, don't you think?How about Your Purpose?Have you ever stopped to think, Why am I here? Or do you ever feel lost, as if something is missing in your life?

When you unlock your creative potential and find clarity in your passion and purpose, success is guaranteed. You can improve your career, financial situation, relationships, health and build unshakable confidence. Your purpose is the driving force that connects you to something larger, something that will allow you to make your mark in this world, to truly make a difference. It is your unique lens through which your brain views the world that shapes your reality. You will know when you are on purpose, you will feel the passion soar through you to the point where you can't sleep and all you want to do is that very thing. Finding your passion and purpose is what sets you on your path to your life and business adventures.

Every individual has gifts and talents that can make a lasting impact. However, only a minority of people utilize those gifts and talents to live up to their full potential. Tying your gifts and talents with your personal purpose not only leads to a more successful career, but a significant one. Many Boomers, as they begin to approach the end of their career, are looking for greater significance. Interestingly, many Millennials, at the other end of their careers, are also looking for significance right out of the gate. As leaders, helping others find their passions and help them have significance at work are becoming bigger parts of our job. And as Millennials continue to make up an increasing part of our workforce, this trend will only become more important. Purpose, passion and performance Purpose, the substrate from which your passions are created, is an important factor in your success at work, a fact that is true even if you don't feel that you can accurately describe your purpose at this moment. To better understand it, look to the things that have captured your imagination or curiosity. Think back to the qualities of assignments that you've found most fulfilling.

What are the common threads that you see? What passions were you exhibiting at those times? Using your passions as a compass to better understand your purpose allows you to leverage them for future success. Doing so is important because research shows that purpose is what allows us to exhibit perseverance or grit -- the willingness to move forward despite difficulties or setbacks, the determination to commit ourselves to a goal. When we are firmly operating within the zone of our purpose, the passions we express are the visible demonstration of our deepest beliefs about the role we are meant to play in the world. Collectively, purpose and passion provide the fuel we need to pursue our goals, professional and personal, even when the path to achieving them isn't easy. Many people have a wrong idea of what constitutes true happiness. It is not attained through self-gratification, but through fidelity to a worthy purpose." In a self-made organization, one that emerges from the grassroots, where the milestones for the first few years are just survival, with time, the purpose often gets diluted. This usually occurs due to a lack of sound fundamentals, or the lack of attention to basics.

Even singly, these two, passion and purpose are extremely potent tools to build sound life basics, but used together - it can make your life completely unassailable. Firm belief in your vision and using the tenets of Passion and Purpose are only a start point. To make ensure a working model, this vision must percolate from the top and carried forth in every action of your life. The advantages of starting from the grassroots cannot be understated. It is like having a blank canvas, lots & lots of paint and your creativity. Let not your passion to colour the canvas use up all the paint, and neither let not your purpose to paint, curb your creativity. Using a judicious mix of the two, think as Da Vinci would before he painted the Madonna or Michealangelo would before he changed a block of stone to into a stunningly life-like image of David. Let this guide you and you will not only see your lifegrow and flourish, but you will see a haloed aura about yourself that attracts people and clients to your business.

HOW TO FIND YOUR PURPOSE?

Have you ever asked yourself what your true purpose in life is? Or do you believe in the purpose of your life in the first place? While some live a rather happy-go-lucky carefree life, there are also some who have been wondering and wandering to find the real reason of their existence. For them, it would seem like there is no meaning to their existence. They would like to find the very reason why they are here in the first place. Finding your purpose is not as easy as it sounds. It cannot just be solved by a mathematical equation, or ruled by a scientific explanation. It is a search within your own self. It is enigmatic. It is mysterious. Most of all, it will require understanding and acceptance. It is not going to be an easy task. It is going to be something that you need patience to get. So what do you do to find your purpose in life? While there are many ways to discover it, there are some things you must remember if you are committed to this search. The biggest thing to arm yourself with is belief. You have to believe that you will be able to find your purpose. Finding your purpose" is more than just a cliché or a dream that will never be fulfilled. It's actually a tool for better, happier, healthier life that too few people attempt to use.

1) Why You Want This in the First Place?

Ultimately you're trying to improve your life and live a meaningful life. You want more zest, more flavor, more fullness. In the strictest sense you want to become a better person. You want to wake up in the morning excited, jumping out of bed with a thirst for life that you haven't felt since you were a child. Your purpose can be the driving force of this. Your purpose can be your connection to something larger, something that will allow you to make your mark on the world, to truly make a difference. Still, your WHY might be different. Before we even leave solid ground you need this as your anchor, just in case things get a little foggy. To find it just answer this question: Why do you want to find your purpose in life?

Write down or remember whatever comes up. It might be some of the above reasons or it might be something entirely different. Whatever it is cherish it, nothing is too far left field.

2) Donate Time, Money, or Talent:

If there's just one habit you can create to help you find your purpose, it would be helping others. Researchers at Florida State University and Stanford found that happiness and meaningfulness had overlap but were different: Happiness was linked to being a taker before a giver, whereas meaningfulness went more with being a giver than a taker. Being the "giver" in a relationship connected people with having a more purposeful life. Altruistic behaviors could include volunteering for a nonprofit organization, donating money to causes you care about, or simply helping out the people around you on a day-to-day basis. Whether you decide to spend two Saturdays a month serving meals in a soup kitchen, or you volunteer to drive your elderly neighbor to the grocery store once a week, doing something kind for others can make you feel as though your life has meaning.

3) **Listen to Feedback:**

It can be hard to recognize the things you feel passionate about sometimes. After all, you probably like to do many different things and the things you love to do may have become so ingrained in your life that you don't realize how important those things are. Fortunately, other people might be able to give you some insight. There's a good chance you're already displaying your passion and purpose to those around you without even realizing it. You might choose to reach out to people and ask what reminds them of you or what they think of when you enter their mind. Or you might take note when someone pays you a compliment or makes an observation about you. Write those observations down and look for patterns. Whether people think of you as "a great entertainer" or they say "you have a passion for helping the elderly," hearing others say what they notice about you might reinforce some of the passions you've already been engaging in.

4) **Explore Your Interests:**

Is there a topic that you are regularly talking about in a Facebook status update or in a Tweet? Are you regularly sharing articles about climate change or refugees? Are there pictures on Instagram of you engaging in a particular activity over and over, such as gardening or performing? Consider the conversations you enjoy holding with people the most when you're meeting face-to-face. Do you like talking about history? Or do you prefer sharing the latest money-saving tips you discovered? The things you like to talk about and the things you enjoy sharing on social media may reveal the things that give you purpose in life.

5) **Surround Yourself With Positive People:**

As the saying goes, you are the company you keep. What do you have in common with the people who you choose to be around? Don't think about co-workers or family members you feel obligated to see. Think about the people you choose to spend time with outside of work and outside of family functions. The people you surround yourself with say something about you. If you're surrounded by people who are making positive change, you might draw from their inspiration. On the other hand, if the people around you are negative individuals who drag you down, you might want to make some changes. It's hard to feel passionate and purposeful when you're surrounded by people who aren't interested in making positive contributions.

6) **Align Your Goals With Your Life Purpose and Passions:**

We're all gifted with a set of talents and interests that tell us what we're supposed to be doing. Once you know what your life purpose is, organize all of your activities around it. Everything you do should be an expression of your purpose. If an activity or goal doesn't fit that formula, don't work on it. Aligning with your purpose is most critical when setting professional goals. When it comes to personal goals, you have more flexibility. If you want to learn how to paint or water ski, go ahead and do so.

CHAPTER 7

OUTSOURCE

Outsourcing is the practice of passing individual tasks, subareas, or business processes over to a third-party and thereby receiving the results from outside of your own company. Services that your company was responsible for fulfilling will now be provided by a specialized service provider. These tasks are often a business's secondary functions: tasks that must be fulfilled in order for a company to focus on its central activity.

WHAT IS OUTSOURCING?

The term "outsourcing" refers to a strategy whereby corporate tasks and structures are given to an external contractor. These can be individual tasks, specific areas, or entire business processes. Outsourcing is a business practice in which services or job functions are farmed out to a third party. In information technology, an outsourcing initiative with a technology provider can involve a range of operations, from the entirety of the IT function to discrete, easily defined components, such as disaster recovery, network services, software development or QA testing. With outsourcing, one or more tasks or processes are usually given to an external partner. Under certain circumstances, however, some tasks be performed internally (in-house outsourcing). For example, if you have given a task to a different area of your company, or to a department which specializes in it, this is commonly known as internal outsourcing. In contrast, a task given in its entirety to an outside company is known as external outsourcing. The external company may be based regionally or may be a foreign contractor. The focus is on potential cost savings. Companies may choose to outsource IT services onshore (within their own country), nearshore (to a neighboring country or one in the same time zone), or offshore (to a more distant country). Nearshore and offshore outsourcing have traditionally been pursued to save costs. Whether you're a business startup, a small enterprise, solo entrepreneur, or just plain hardworking person who wants everything done in no time at all, maximizing your time is possible. The solution? Outsourcing.

BENEFITS OF OUTSOURCING

Outsourcing occurs when a company purchases products or services from an outside supplier, rather than performing the same work within its own facilities, in order to cut costs. The decision to outsource is a major strategic one for most companies, since it involves weighing the potential cost savings against the consequences of a loss in control over the product or service. Some common examples of outsourcing include manufacturing of components, computer programming services, tax compliance and other accounting functions, training administration, customer service, transportation of products, benefits and compensation planning, payroll, and other human resource functions. A relatively new trend in outsourcing is employee leasing, in which specialized vendors recruit, hire, train, and pay their clients' employees, as well as arrange health care coverage and other benefits.

1) **Promote Growth:**

The overhead costs of some operations are extremely high, but you might want to offer them to satisfy customers, expand your business model, or compete in the marketplace. Outsourcing can be a good option if the cost of expanding to handle those operations yourself is too expensive, would take too long to effect, or would create inefficiencies in your business model. For instance, your small doctor's office wants to accept a variety of insurance plans, but one staff member can't keep up with all the different providers and rules. Outsourcing to a firm that specializes in medical billing will cost less than hiring additional skilled staff or training existing personnel, while still increasing the benefit to your customers.

2) **You Can Focus On Core Areas:**

It's been known that the quality of core activities suffers as a business grows. Outsourcing your business tasks would free your time and energies and enable you to focus on building your brand, invest in research and development and create new ways of providing higher value-added services.

3) **Freeing Up Internal Resources:**

Why waste people in areas that don't focus on core business functions? Capital and people are becoming higher commodities in a difficult financial environment, and companies need as many good people as possible to focus on what really matters with a business. By outsourcing lesser services, companies free up time and capital to move their business forward.

4) **Maintain Lower Costs:**

Sometimes the expense of purchasing equipment or needing a new location can be prohibitive. In these cases, it's more cost-effective to outsource than to expand operations internally. If the growth of your business results in an increased need for office space, try outsourcing simple operations such as telemarketing or data entry rather than moving to a new location. It might cost far less than the price of expanding, and it is both more efficient and less expensive than relocating. Outsourcing can also lower costs by reducing the expenses associated with bringing on new employees, such as:

- A hiring search

- Onboarding

- Healthcare and other benefits

- Payroll taxes

- Increased need for workers in management and HR positions

Working with contractors rather than employees can minimize these costs, allowing your business to get the same amount done for less.

6) You Save More:

Access to cheaper labor is probably the most well-known reason businesses consider outsourcing. Workers in developing countries are paid far less than workers in established and flourishing countries due to the lower cost of living. This allows your business to get the work done for a fraction of the price. Not to mention relieving you of paying expensive benefits since the outside firm takes on this responsibility.

7) You Have Access To Better Technology:

If you have a small business, chances are you can't afford to provide all your employees with the latest technology. Outsourcing helps you solve this because service providers can afford the latest technology since it's part of their core business. More importantly, having the latest in technology to use helps your business to perform processes at an optimum rate, and thus be profitable.

REASONS FOR OUTSOURCING

There are numerous reasons for outsourcing some types of work functions. Business owners and corporations choose this option as a way to save money in company operations, maneuver the company into a more competitive position, and to solve manpower issues without the cost of hiring more employees.

1) **Costs:**

One of the main advantages of outsourcing processes certainly is the emerging cost advantage. This can be traced back to several reasons. Outsourcing within one's own economic area already facilitates savings in a double-digit realm; outsourcing to other countries often entails an even larger cost advantage. For instance, external service providers often can resort to specialized technologies respectively infrastructures or they have better trade agreements or labour costs. Furthermore, costs only arise when a project is being processed. If occasionally the services of the external service provider are not required, no costs arise either. Even for smaller businesses this pays off. The working hours a managing director spends on tasks, for instance, which are not really part of his core competence, are quite costly and not really efficient compared to outsourcing these tasks and thus freeing the managing director to direct his attention to his tasks.

2) **Flexibility:**

With uncertainty surrounding today's global economy, companies need the ability to expand or downsize quickly. Unfortunately, that's not always possible with today's labor laws, as employee lawsuits are at an all-time high. By outsourcing, companies take that risk away, allowing businesses to adapt more quickly to rising or slowing demand. On the one hand the tasks, which have to be handled in the short term, can be promptly outsourced, which creates additional resources during peak times of the business. This way it can be guaranteed that during seasonal additional workloads or during strong growth periods nobody from the permanent staff will be overburdened. In case of unforeseen tasks, single projects or processes can be outsourced to service providers and thus time capacities be freed to meet the sudden demands.

3) **Access To A Larger Talent Pool:**

When hiring an employee, you may only have access to a small, local talent pool. This often means you have to compromise. Many companies have found that outsourcing gives them access to talent in other parts of the world. If you need specialized help, it often makes sense to expand your search.The advantage of outsourcing is also the access to a vast portfolio of specialized people. A company can co-operate for the time being on a project basis with a partner, who is a specialist in one area of expertise, but who would otherwise not stand a chance to gain a steady employment in this company due to his/her high specialisation. Thus, outsourcing renders more advantages than merely saving costs and is therefore not only interesting for large enterprises, but especially for smaller and medium-sized businesses, too.

4) **Concetration on essentials:**

If you outsource processes, which are outside your competence, and pass them on to adequate specialists, you can fully concentrate on their actual tasks again. This has the noticeable advantage that business can be further promoted and the – financial and time – advantages thus gained, be used at other places in a sensible or profitable way. Nobody likes to struggle with tasks for which one lacks the competence, while work, that pushes the business forward, is neglected. This way, one can target in on one's own area of expertise and thus work out a ledge compared to the competition.

5) Swiftness:

Tasks which are rarely handled or for which the necessary know-how must be acquired first, can be handled much more efficiently by outsourcing. After all, external experts finish the tasks in their specific areas of expertise as a routine task and thus have optimized the required processes in regard to time and effort. Furthermore, they are oftentimes more flexible and can – if need be – swiftly be instructed to handle tasks.

CONCLUSION

Your intense desire to succeed cause you to change the status quo. It helps you start and motivates you to endure in the face of obstacles. it's what permits one to beat overwhelming odds. Once you create that burning obsession, you'll do whatever it takes to realize that goal. You'll invest all of your time, energy and self into attaining what you want. Failure may be inevitable in life, but as long as we keep trying, it is only part of the process, not the endpoint. We can stay with broken technology and methodology and remain in a rut of our own devising, or we can consider failure a positive force for change. We can reimagine how we do things— from high-tech gadgets to the way we live our lives and structure our societies. Succeeding is not about avoiding failure but about learning from our mistakes and moving forward.

www.ingramcontent.com/pod-product-compliance
Lightning Source LLC
Chambersburg PA
CBHW020604220526
45463CB00006B/2446